O9-AIG-187

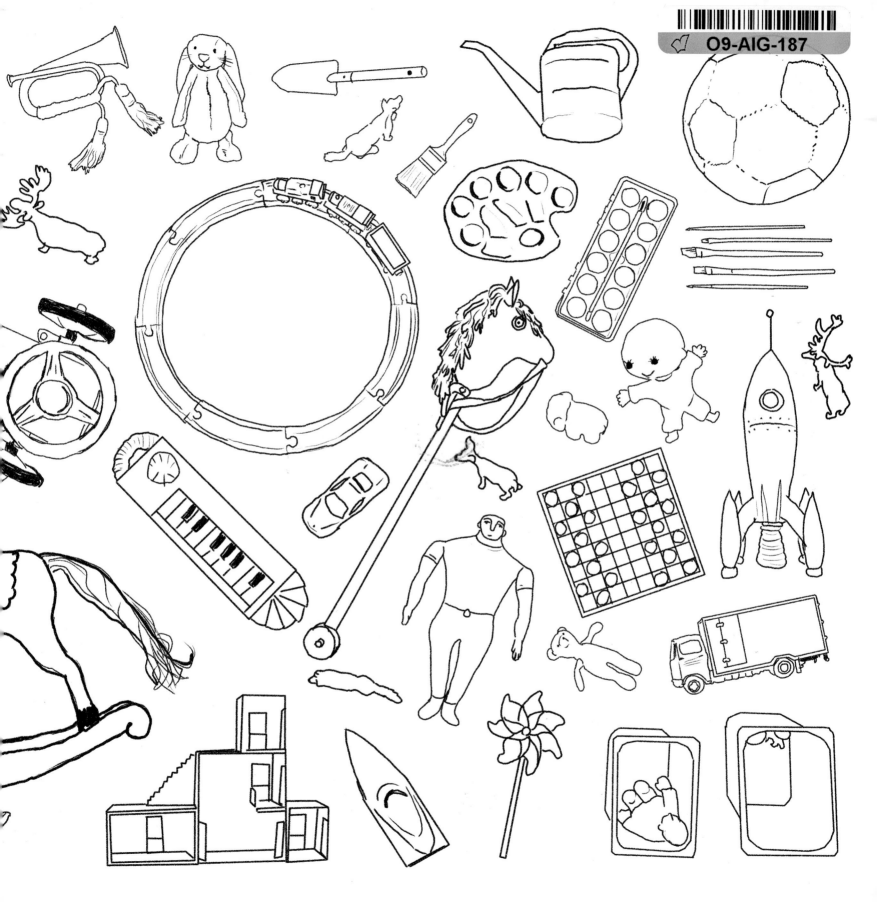

who
are
you?

First published in 2017
by Jessica Kingsley Publishers
73 Collier Street
London N1 9BE, UK
and
400 Market Street, Suite 400
Philadelphia, PA 19106, USA

www.jkp.com

Copyright © Brook Pessin-Whedbee 2017
Illustrations copyright © Naomi Bardoff 2017

All rights reserved. No part of this publication may be reproduced
in any material form (including photocopying, storing in any
medium by electronic means or transmitting) without the written
permission of the copyright owner except in accordance with
the provisions of the law or under terms of a licence issued in
the UK by the Copyright Licensing Agency Ltd. www.cla.co.uk
or in overseas territories by the relevant reproduction rights
organisation, for details see www.ifrro.org. Applications for the
copyright owner's written permission to reproduce any part of this
publication should be addressed to the publisher.

Warning: The doing of an unauthorised act in relation to a
copyright work may result in both a civil claim for damages and
criminal prosecution.

Library of Congress Cataloging in Publication Data
A CIP catalog record for this book is available from the
Library of Congress

British Library Cataloguing in Publication Data
A CIP catalogue record for this book is available from the
British Library

ISBN 978 1 78592 728 7

Printed and bound in China

who are you?

the kid's guide to gender identity

Brook Pessin-Whedbee
Illustrated by Naomi Bardoff

Jessica Kingsley Publishers
London and Philadelphia

Dedicated to all the little people with big hearts and curious minds,
especially Rosa Parks Elementary, Class of 2018.

This book was inspired by the groundbreaking work of Gender Spectrum and was made possible by support from their incredible team, especially Pam Wool, Mere Abrams, Joel Baum, and Stephanie Brill. Many thanks as well to the trailblazing educators who create communities that celebrate diversity, especially Kim Beeson, Michelle Contreras, and all the amazing folks in Berkeley, Oakland, and Los Angeles.

This book would not have come to be without the contributions and advice from so many others, including Nina Pessin-Whedbee, Tamar Beja, Sam Lopes, Kirsty White, Sumita Soni, Stacey Lewis, Jon Nicols, Innosanto Nagara, and Rick Oculto.

I am also grateful for the generous support and loving encouragement from The Whedbee/Yoritomos, The Pessins, The Carlises, The Wangskis and, especially, Micah, Aniela, Rosalia, and Drew.

A Note for the Grown-Ups

This is a book about all of us. From the moment we are born, and often even before that, people talk about gender. It is one of many things that make us individuals in the world—we each have our own unique web that includes our body, how we feel inside, and how we express ourselves. Gender is individual, and it is also something that connects us to the people around us.

People experience gender in so many ways. Some grown-ups may worry that children are too young to talk about gender diversity. But it is all around us. Kids are already talking about it, and you get to decide how you want to be a part of that conversation. For some, reading this book with a little person in your life may be the first explicit discussion you have had about gender. For others, it is part of a bigger conversation that may have begun days or months or years ago.

Either way, it is a good idea to first read this book to yourself, or even with other grown-ups. You might also like to take a look at the guide at the back of the book, or go to our website: kidsguidetogender.com. There, you will find answers to common questions, information on key concepts, things to point out or ask as you read, and additional resources.

This book is meant as a tool to be used alongside the rainbow of other great resources out there in the world—there are so many books, websites and organizations that offer great stories, perspectives and information. Of course, if you have questions or ideas you'd like to share with me, please do! I'm happy to share my experiences and connect you with some of the amazing folks out there.

Gender is personal. Every reader, from age 1 to 101, will have a connection to this book. I encourage you to think about what makes this personal for you and to share that with the little people in your life. I encourage you to ask questions about what makes this personal for them. You may be surprised and delighted by how much they have to say.

I hope you will read this book over and over again with the little ones in your life. It will be a new experience each time!

Brook

The important thing to remember
is that you are the one
who knows you best.

When babies are born, people ask...

"Is it a boy or a girl?"

Babies can't talk, so grown-ups make
a guess by looking at their bodies.

This is the sex assigned to you at birth,
male or female.

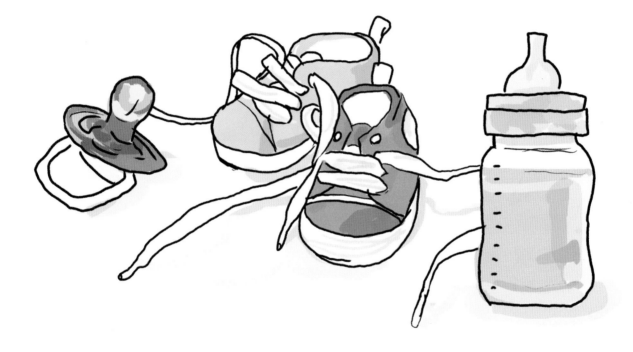

Sometimes people get this confused with gender.
But gender is much more than the body you were born with.

As babies grow into kids, they start to know what they like and don't like.

8

This is your personal expression –
what you like, how you dress and act.

There are so many ways to express yourself!
What you like can change as you grow up,
or even from day to day!

What do you like?

13

Kids know a lot about themselves.
They know who they are by how
they feel inside.

This is your identity – who you feel
like inside, who you know yourself
to be. This can also change as you
grow up, or change from day to day!
Your gender is just one part of your
identity, what makes you YOU.

Some people say there are only two genders.
But there are really many genders.

I am...
girl   boy
both   neither
JUST
ME!
_____
_____

You are who you say you are,
because YOU know you best.

For some people, the grown-ups guessed right about their body and their gender.

This is called cisgender – when someone's identity matches their sex assigned at birth.

19

And for some people, there are more than just two choices.

These are just a few words people use: trans, genderqueer, non-binary, gender fluid, transgender, gender neutral, agender, neutrois, bigender, third gender, two-spirit...

...and there are even more words people are using to describe their experience.

This is called the gender spectrum.

There are lots of ways to be a boy.

There are lots of ways to be a girl.

There are lots of ways to be a kid.

BE WHO YOU ARE!

Guide for Grown-Ups

Gender diversity is about human diversity. Ideally, before reading this book with the little people in your life, you will have laid a foundation for understanding and celebrating differences and individuality. This book is not meant to be the starting point, but, rather, a tool to delve deeper into a conversation that has already begun.

Particularly if you are reading this with a class or a group of children, it is important to find age-appropriate ways to discuss stereotyping and the boxes that exist for boys and girls. These are just a few of the great books and activities you might start with:

- Read *It's Ok to Be Different* by Todd Parr. What makes you special and proud of yourself? (Ages 3–8)

- Watch music video *I Am Me* by Willow Smith and read Walter Dean Myers' *Looking Like Me* to explore identity through song and poetry. What makes you unique? (Ages 6–10)

- Read *The Story of Ferdinand* by Munro Leaf or other books that challenge gender stereotypes. Tell the story of a 6-year-old who likes both stereotypically "boy" things and stereotypically "girl" things, but doesn't feel like a boy *or* a girl. Have you ever felt like that? What stereotypes do we have for boys and girls? (Ages 3–10)

- Listen to the MOSAIC Project song *Dance and Be Free* and show the Gender Spectrum *Think Outside the Boxes* poster. Have you ever felt like the kids in the song? What boxes exist for boys and girls? (Ages 6–10)

- Read *Red: A Crayon's Story* by Michael Hall. Have you ever heard any of the comments the crayons make? Have you ever felt like red? (Ages 3–10)

- Listen to the song and read the book *All I Want to Be is Me* by Phyllis Rothblatt. (Ages 3–10)

Links to all of these resources and much more can be found at our website: kidsguidetogender.com

A Page-by-Page Guide to Key Concepts and Discussion Points

If talking about gender with kids is new to you, the background information in this section may help, as you read the book. You will also find ideas for questions to ask and things to point out.

Body (Pages 4–7)

**When babies are born...
gender is much more than the
body you were born with.**

You might ask... Do you know any babies who have been born? What did people say about them? Where have you heard the words male and female before?

You might also point out... It is important to be respectful when talking about bodies. This means not asking people about their body unless they tell you they are comfortable talking about it.

More information: Sex is a word with several meanings. In this case, it refers to the body we are born with, including external sex organs, sex chromosomes, hormones, and internal reproductive structures. People are assigned a sex when they are born, and sometimes even before they are born. Most of the time, someone looks at a baby's body and decides, "It's a boy!" or "It's a girl." We usually only hear about two options—male or female—but some of us are born with bodies that don't fit this binary. These variations are called intersex, which means "between the sexes" and there are a lot of ways that can look. So even though most people have bodies that are typically assigned "male" or "female," sex is actually more of a spectrum with a range of natural variation.

Expression (Pages 8–10)

**As babies grow into kids...
What do you like?**

You might ask... Have the things you like changed since you were younger? Are there things you like sometimes but not other times? Have you ever heard someone talk about "boy" clothes/hair/toys/colors or "girl" clothes/hair/toys/colors? What do you think about that? How does that make you feel?

You might also point out... Clothes are just clothes, toys are just toys, hair is just hair, colors are just colors. We should all get to wear/play with /like what makes us feel good. We should all feel proud of what we like because that's what makes us unique! There are lots of things that can cause others to make assumptions about us: hair, clothing, accessories, toys, activities, mannerisms, and behavior. We can also think about the assumptions we make about others.

More information: Gender stereotypes are constantly changing. Today, blue is sometimes considered a "boy" color and pink a "girl" color. Years ago, it was the opposite. In 1918, an Earnshaw's Infants' Department article said, "The generally accepted rule is pink for the boys, and blue for the girls. The reason is that pink, being a more decided and stronger color, is more suitable for the boy, while blue, which is more delicate and dainty, is prettier for the girl." Today, we see women wearing jeans and men with earrings, but those were not always socially accepted styles. Times have changed and will continue to change. But, regardless of stereotypes, what we like does not determine our gender identity.

Identity (Page 15)

Kids know a lot about themselves... what makes you YOU.

You might ask... Who are you? What makes you YOU? How do you know? Has this changed since you were younger?

You might also point out... Who we are—our identity—is made up of so many different parts: language, race, ethnicity, family background, gender, interests, and so much more. These parts all intersect in complicated ways that make us each our own unique person. And our concept of ourselves can change as we develop and grow.

Gender diversity (Pages 16–21)

Some people say there are only two genders. ... This is called the gender spectrum.

You might ask... Who are you? Are there other words you use to describe yourself? Are there other words you have heard people use to describe themselves?

You might also point out... Being respectful means believing people when they say who they are and calling them what they prefer to be called. People use all kinds of pronouns, like she/her/hers, he/him/his, they/them/their, ze/hir/hirs, and more. Sometimes, people prefer no pronoun at all. If you're not sure what name or pronoun someone prefers, just ask!

More information: Gender diversity is not a new concept. Cultures around the world and throughout history have recognized more than two genders. The words we use to describe ourselves are changing all the time. Definitions also change, and mean different things to different people. You can learn a lot by just asking, "What does that word mean to you?" The important thing to remember is that everyone has a story and each of us has a unique way of saying who we are.

About The Interactive Wheel

There are lots of models for visually representing gender, from a simple binary of two boxes to a tangled ball of yarn. We chose the wheel because the concentric circles capture the complex and layered nature and the endless possibilities of gender. While this book is all about breaking down binary notions of gender, this tool is still limited as it offers a finite number of categories for concepts that are, in fact, much more complex. On all three layers, there may be more than one choice that resonates with you. We hope that you will use this tool as a scaffold to show the infinite possibilities for how people experience gender.

The Body Wheel

We simplified this concept into three main groups, but there is a lot of natural variation within each category. If it seems appropriate, you can name specific body parts and other features with your kids. Just as toys are just toys and clothes are just clothes...bodies are just bodies!

The Identity Wheel

Gender identity is so individual that this layer could include only one choice: "I am just me!" But this model offers a scaffold for those who are just beginning to understand gender. Beyond the "boy/girl" binary, there are many different ways to feel. (And sometimes, we are not sure, and that's okay too!) We included just some of the many words we can use to describe ourselves—the list goes on and is constantly changing. The blank space is for your own words.

The Expression Wheel

There are so many things to like in the world, we could not possibly include them all. The blank space is for whatever you like that is missing from the list.

*A note on perspective: The wheel is presented in the first person ("I have... I am... I like...") because *you* are the one who knows you best. And we don't know about other people unless they tell us. For some little people, however, it might feel difficult at first to talk about themselves. In this case, you might try to reframe this in a more general way ("Some people have...feel like...like...") and explore different possibilities until they find something that resonates with them.

Additional Resources

Visit our website: kidsguidetogender.com for links to all of these resources and much more!

Books and Films that Tell a Personal Story

Because gender is such an individual thing, one way to help little people understand the diversity of experience is through personal stories. You may like to use The Gender Wheel alongside these stories, mapping different ways people experience gender. This is only a starting point—there are so many new stories being shared each day!

These are just a few of the many terrific books exploring gender diversity:

- Barbara E. Barber, *Allie's Basketball Dream*

- Mary Hoffman, *Amazing Grace*

- Mayra L. Dole, *Drum, Chavi, Drum! / ¡Toca, Chavi, toca!*

- Jessica Herthel and Jazz Jennings, *I am Jazz*

- Christine Baldachinno, *Morris Micklewhite and the Tangerine Dress*

- Laurin Mayeno, *One of a Kind, Like Me / Único Como Yo*

These documentaries and films highlight some of the brave youth who are telling their stories:

- *A Place in the Middle* (2014)

- *Becoming Johanna* (2016)

- *I'm Just Anneke* (2010)

- *Tomgirl* (2015)

- *Growing Up Trans* (2015)

- *Kuma Hina* (2014)

- *Ma Vie en Rose* (1997)

- *Next Goal Wins* (2014)

- *Tomboy* (2011)

You might also like to share the stories of LGBTQ role models such as Maria Munir, Jazz Jennings, Willow Smith, Brendan Jordan, Nicole Mains, Tyler Ford, and more!

Books for Grown-ups Supporting Gender Expansive Youth

- Stephanie A. Brill and Rachel Pepper, *The Transgender Child: A Handbook for Families and Professionals*

- Diane Ehrensaft, *The Gender Creative Child: Pathways for Nurturing and Supporting Children Who Live Outside Gender Boxes*

- Amy Ellis Nutt, *Becoming Nicole: The Transformation of an American Family*

- Lori Duron, *Raising My Rainbow: Adventures in Raising a Fabulous Gender Creative Son*

Organizations Offering Additional Resources

- Gender Spectrum (www.genderspectrum.org)

- Welcoming Schools (www.welcomingschools.org)

- Human Rights Campaign (www.hrc.org)

- Mermaids (www.mermaidsuk.org.uk)

- PFLAG (www.pflag.org)

- The Gay, Lesbian & Straight Education Network (www.glsen.org)

- Trans Student Education Resources (www.transstudent.org)

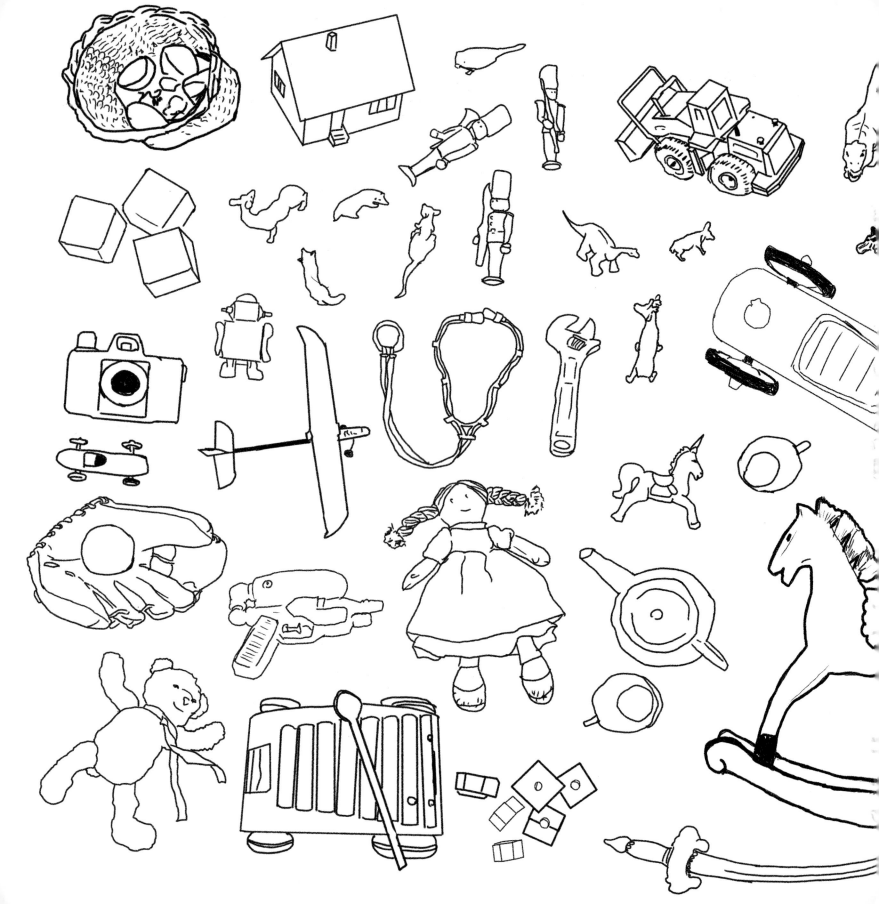